W9-AZW-157

Does it sink or float?

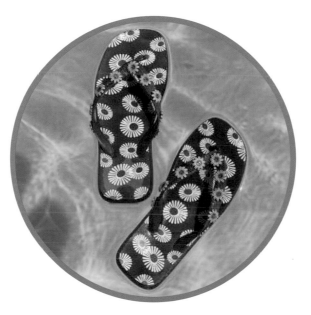

Susan Hughes

Crabtree Publishing Company

www.crabtreebooks.com

What's the Matter?

Author: Susan Hughes
Publishing plan research and development:
 Reagan Miller
Project development: Clarity Content Services
Project management: Joanne Chan
Project coordinator: Kathy Middleton
Editors: Joanne Chan, Reagan Miller
Copy editor: Dimitra Chronopoulos
Proofreader: Kelly Spence, Kylie Korneluk
Design: Pixel Hive studio
Photo research: Linda Tanaka
Production coordinator and
 prepress technician: Tammy McGarr
Print coordinator: Margaret Amy Salter

Photographs:
Cover Shutterstock; p1 Kameel4u/Shutterstock; p4 top
Kyslynskyy/Thinkstock, joyfnp/Thinkstock; p5 Polka
Dot/Thinkstock; p6 Vesna Cvorovic/Thinkstock; p7 Andrey
Guryanov/Thinkstock; p8 top Alleyn Plowright/Thinkstock; p9 Getty
Images/Thinkstock, Monkey Business Images/Shutterstock; p10 top
Getty Images/Thinkstock, targovcom/Thinkstock; p11 Elena
Elisseeva/Thinkstock; p12 top Fernando Gregory Milan/Thinkstock,
Greg Epperson/Thinkstock; p13 left Valentinash/Shutterstock, Ugo
Montaldo/Shutterstock; p14 David Tanaka; p15 top David Tanaka,
fotofermer/Thinkstock; p16 top JkovAlex/Thinkstock, Stefan
Pircher/Shutterstock; p17 top Alta Oosthuizen/Thinkstock,
Phoenixman/Thinkstock; p18 top Digital Vision/Thinkstock, Getty
Images/Thinkstock; p19 iurli/Shutterstock; p20 David Tanaka; p21 top
David Tanaka, Kameel4u/Shutterstock; p22 top left mercedes
rancaño/Thinkstock, Stockbyte/Thinkstock, Palle
Christensen/Thinkstock, bottom Mega Pixel/Shutterstock.

Library and Archives Canada Cataloguing in Publication

Hughes, Susan, 1960-, author
 Does it sink or float? / Susan Hughes.

(What's the matter?)
Includes index.
Issued in print and electronic formats.
ISBN 978-0-7787-0536-9 (bound).--ISBN 978-0-7787-0540-6 (pbk.).--
ISBN 978-1-4271-9025-3 (html).--ISBN 978-1-4271-9029-1 (pdf)

 1. Specific gravity--Juvenile literature. 2. Matter--Properties--
Juvenile literature. I. Title. II. Series: What's the matter?
(St. Catharines, Ont.)

QC111.H85 2014   j531'.14   C2014-900449-4
                                          C2014-900450-8

Library of Congress Cataloging-in-Publication Data

Hughes, Susan, 1960- author.
 Does it sink or float? / Susan Hughes.
  pages cm. -- (What's the matter?)
Audience: 5-8.
Audience: K to Grade 3.
Includes bibliographical references and index.
 ISBN 978-0-7787-0536-9 (reinforced library binding : alk. paper) -- ISBN 978-0-
7787-0540-6 (pbk. : alk. paper) -- ISBN 978-1-4271-9025-3 (electronic html) --
ISBN 978-1-4271-9029-1 (electronic pdf)
 1. Floating bodies--Juvenile literature. 2. Matter--Properties--Juvenile
literature. I. Title.

QC147.5.H84 2015
531'.54--dc23
                          2014002264

Crabtree Publishing Company

www.crabtreebooks.com   1-800-387-7650

Printed in Canada/052018/MQ20180424

Copyright © **2014 CRABTREE PUBLISHING COMPANY**. All rights reserved. No part of this publication may be reproduced, stored in a retrieval system
or be transmitted in any form or by any means, electronic, mechanical, photocopying, recording, or otherwise, without the prior written permission of Crabtree
Publishing Company. In Canada: We acknowledge the financial support of the Government of Canada through the Canada Book Fund for our publishing activities.

Published in Canada
Crabtree Publishing
616 Welland Ave.
St. Catharines, ON
L2M 5V6

Published in the United States
Crabtree Publishing
PMB 59051
350 Fifth Avenue, 59th Floor
New York, New York 10118

Published in the United Kingdom
Crabtree Publishing
Maritime House
Basin Road North, Hove
BN41 1WR

Published in Australia
Crabtree Publishing
3 Charles Street
Coburg North
VIC 3058

What is in this book?

What is matter? 4

What are properties? 6

Float or sink? 8

Does it float? 10

Does it sink? 12

Why do things sink or float? 14

High density or low density? 16

Just add air 18

Get in shape! 20

Float or sink quiz 22

Words to know and Index 23

Notes for adults 24

What is matter?

All objects are made of **matter**.

Matter is anything that takes up space and has **mass**.

Mass is the amount of material in an object.

A tiger, flowers, and everything you see around you is made of matter.

You are made
of matter, too!

What are properties?

Matter has **properties**. Properties describe how something looks, feels, tastes, smells, or sounds.

We can taste this lemon to learn if it is sweet or sour. Sweet and sour are properties that describe how something tastes.

We can look at this Ferris wheel to learn about its shape. Shape is a property, too.

Float or sink?

Properties also describe how something acts. An object can **float** or **sink** depending on what material it is made of. For example, some things float, or stay on top of a liquid such as water.

Other things
sink, or fall
to the bottom
of a liquid.

Objects that float
are described as
buoyant.

Buoyancy is a
property of
matter.

Does it float?

Rubber ducks float. They are fun bath toys!

Water wings float. This girl is wearing water wings on her arms. They can help her learn to swim.

Canoes float. People use them to travel over lakes, rivers, and oceans.

Why do all of these objects need to float?

Does it sink?

An object sinks or floats depending on its properties.

An anchor sinks so it can keep a boat in one place.

Stones sink. We use them to make stepping stones across water.

A net sinks. People use them to catch fish. Some nets have floaters to keep them from sinking to the bottom of the ocean.

Why do all of these objects need to sink?

Why do things sink or float?

Objects are made of materials which have **density**. Density is a measure of how closely together matter is packed.

An object with low density floats in water. It is made of material that is less dense than water.

This lid floats because plastic is less dense than water.

An object with high density sinks in water. It is made of material that is denser than water. These coins sink because metal is denser than water.

Wood is a material that is less dense than water. Would a toothpick float or sink in water? How do you know?

High density or low density?

Rocks are denser than water. Rocks sink.

Objects made of metal usually sink. A steel diving cage sinks.

A feather is less dense than water. It floats.

A lilypad floats on water. It is less dense than water.

Just add air

Some objects have air in them. This helps them float.

A rubber boat floats.

So does a beach ball.

A submarine has special compartments, or sections.

When they are filled with water, the submarine is denser than water. It sinks.

When the compartments are filled with air, the submarine rises. Now it has less density than water.

? What would happen if you put an empty bottle in water? What if you filled it with sand?

Get in shape!

The shape of an object can help it float or sink.

A flat piece of plasticine floats.

A round, solid ball of plasticine sinks.

Rubber flip-flops float. They are flat.

? Imagine you want to float in water. Will you curl up in a ball or stretch out flat?

Float or sink quiz

Look at these objects. Which objects float and which sink?

A

B

C

D

Answer: A) A life ring floats. B) A hammer sinks. C) Corks float. D) A plate sinks.

Words to know and Index

buoyant page 9

density pages 14–17, 19

float pages 8–11, 14–15, 17–19, 20–21

mass page 4

matter pages 4–5, 9, 14

properties pages 6–9

sink pages 8–9, 12–16, 19–21

Notes for adults

Objectives
- to introduce the difference between objects that float and objects that sink
- to learn about how people use these objects in everyday life

Prerequisite
Ask the children to read *Is it heavy or light?* before reading *Does it sink or float?* Introducing them to the concept of weight with *Is it heavy or light?* will help familiarize them with the initial concepts in this book.

Questions before reading *Does it sink or float?*
"What things sink? What things float?"

"Tell me about a time when you put something in water and it floated."

"How is something that sinks different from something that floats?"

"When would you ever use something that floats?"

Discussion
Read the book with the children. Discuss with the children some of the main concepts in the book, such as float and sink, buoyancy, and density.

Have the children collect small household objects, such as a spoon, a marble, a toothpick, a paper clip, a button, and so on. Ask them to tell whether they think the object will float or sink in water. Ask them to explain their thinking. Have them test their predictions by putting the objects in a sink or pan of water.

Extension
Provide the children with plasticine and a pan of water. Have them experiment to make a "boat" that will float. Ask them to describe the shape of their boat. Have them change the shape to make the boat sink. Have them describe and explain what happened.